To,

DR. YAREMA, STAFF & GUESTS,

With Aloha,

Raj Kumar

12/24/05

Pearls of Wisdom For Everyday Living

By

Raj Kumar, Ph. D.

authorHOUSE™

1663 LIBERTY DRIVE, SUITE 200
BLOOMINGTON, INDIANA 47403
(800) 839-8640
WWW.AUTHORHOUSE.COM

© 2005 Raj Kumar, Ph. D. All Rights Reserved.

No part of this book may be reproduced, stored in a retrieval system, or transmitted by any means without the written permission of the author.

First published by AuthorHouse 11/17/05

ISBN: 1-4208-8110-8 (sc)

Library of Congress Control Number: 2005907801

Printed in the United States of America
Bloomington, Indiana

This book is printed on acid-free paper.

DEDICATION

This book is dedicated to my parents and my loving wife Sunita who has inspired and supported me in all walks of life.

This book is dedicated to Goddess Sarasvati, the mother of love, light, wisdom, and compassion. She has guided me to do meaningful things since my childhood. I feel fortunate to receive her blessings and divine guidance throughout my life. The higher goal of my life is to share knowledge with others.

Satguru Sivaya Subramunia Swami

Finally, this book is also dedicated to my spiritual Master Satguru Sivaya Subramunia Swami, the founder of Kauai temple who passed away in 2001 but his teachings are always alive with us. I have been inspired by his spiritual knowledge, teachings and good deeds for humanity. I moved on a spiritual path after reading his books and the magazine "Hinduism Today."

Raj Kumar

ACKNOWLEDGEMENT

I would like to express my sincere gratitude to the following people:

Mr. Indra Sharma, a famous artist from India for making a special painting for the cover page. Mr. Eric Ryan for creating a beautiful cover.

Mr. Craig Shull and Ms.Caron Wilberts for taking their valuable time to edit this book.

INTRODUCTION

I have written this book based on my practical and spiritual experience in life. Several spiritual masters have blessed me since my childhood. My paternal grandfather and my mother who always involved me in daily prayers, rituals and spiritual practices, influenced me. Since age 10, I learned that I had pre- cognition ability. I started to have special visions and dreams, especially on Monday mornings as I was born on Monday. I was able to tell my friend about future happenings. I would sing a song and 5 minutes later it was playing on the radio. My faith developed and became stronger, when I witnessed and experienced some miracles and when my wishes came true in a short period of time. I grew in the power of self-confidence and faith in God.

I was born with a congenital problem called Atrial Septal defect (a whole in the heart). I lived with this condition for 38 years. In 1998, I felt tremendous pain in my back and went to see different doctors but no one could make a firm diagnosis of my condition. When my cardiologist Dr. Neil Shikuma detected the heart problem, he was surprised to know that I never had any chest pain or blood pressure symptoms. Medical tests such as X ray and EKG could not detect symptoms of a heart problem. He said that patients with a similar condition have died during childhood. My wife took me to a psychic reader at a local bookstore in Hawaii. The Psychic reader immediately pointed out that "you are going through some medical condition and you need surgery". She assured me that everything would be all right, and I would have a new life after the surgery. She said that God had chosen me for a purpose and I would find that purpose after the surgery.

In July 1998, when I was recovering from surgery, I meditated for 5 days in the hospital and I was given the vision through the meditation, that I should go into the healing practice and help others through writing. After publishing 2 books, I have received more grace, love, and compassion from others.

"The richer are not those who have more wealth and material possessions but those who share love and knowledge with others and receive more love, blessings, and support in return."

I do not claim to be the author of this book. I am just an instrument of God and servant to other living beings on the planet. The quotes written in this book have come to me through divine guidance. There are 365 quotes in this book. After each month, there is a blank page "Inner reflections" designed for you to write your spiritual experiences and positive changes so that you can measure your progress towards your goals and destiny. You may find the answers to some of your life's problems in this book. This book guides you to move on a spiritual path. Spiritual journeys begin in different times and different circumstances in our life but whenever it begins, it is never too late as it shifts the consciousness from materialism to spiritualism. This is the right path to experience supreme bliss and feel the presence of God within. Life is an experience of happiness, sadness, pain, and suffering. Every human being has to go through different stages and ups and downs in life based on their Karma. One, who is a good karma yogi, lives in the world but remains detached from material possessions, understands the game of life, lives simply and peacefully, and achieves liberation in this life. My spiritual master said that "Every good advice works, if you believe in that person and practice it sincerely in your daily life." If you do not believe others and feel that you know everything, then nothing works. Be grateful and generous to others. I am advising the readers of this book to start your day with a little prayer in the morning and be mindful throughout the daily activities, and do one good deed for others daily. You will feel great joy in your heart and a deep satisfaction in your life.

"We all have a purpose to come to in this life, one of the major purposes of life is to know thyself and serve others selflessly."

DESTINY

You are the creation of God

You are the reflection of your parents

You are the product of your childhood

You are what you believe

You are what you think

You are what you speak

You are what your association is with others

You are how you act or behave with others

You are what choices you make everyday

You receive what you give to others

You experience what your desires are

What your desires are, so are your deeds

What your deeds are, so is your destiny

JANUARY

1   When you always think of the past, it is possible that the same things may occur and ruin your present. We make our future from the present. If your present is ruined, your future will be ruined also. Release and let go of your past. Enjoy your present, it is your future.

2   If a person can control his/her mind and five senses, he/she can conquer anything in this world. Always listening to and following your mind means being a slave to your mind. Listening to the inner voice means making the right decision in the right situation and for the right purpose.

3   Desires are the cause of sorrows. Do not be tempted by the worldly things or the possessions people have. Be satisfied with whatever you have and accept whatever life offers to you. Even if change, loss, sickness, death, and failure comes your way, know, understand, accept everything and move along with the changes in life.

The acceptance of change will make you strong and will bring you closer to God.

4   One, who recognizes his/her higher self, unfolds the layers of darkness (illusions) through internal knowledge (wisdom) and attains the state of self- realization (God consciousness).

5   The richest person is one who has done more good deeds for others not the one who has more wealth, gold and land. Count your blessings and see how rich you are.

6   Do not worry much about life's problems. Always step back to see and understand what caused the problems. Most of the time, the answer is within you, within the problem, or within your environment. Increase your awareness and insight and take appropriate steps to correct the problems. If you are still unable to resolve your problems then surrender your problem to God and ask for help and solutions with a pure heart. You will be surprised to see that miracles can happen anytime and anywhere.

7   Happiness is a basic state of mind. It manifests itself when the mind is not distracted by temptations and anger, and is totally relaxed. The secrets of happiness are as follows: (I) Find happiness within yourself (II) Choose to be happy. (III) Know the source of happiness in God. (IV) Have a sense of humor. (V) Help poor and needy people. (VI) Share knowledge and love with others. (VII) Clean your cluttered mind and maintain positive thoughts. (VII) Control desires for money, fame, fun, power, and possessions. Live a simple life. (IX) Maintain inner peace through meditation and prayers. (X) Live in the present. (XI) Stay healthy.

8   One of the major goals of every one's life is to serve others and to be served by others selflessly. People come and go in this world but the wisdom and good deeds of great people stay forever.

9   You make appointments to meet others. Have you ever made an appointment with God? When you think and care, God is always there. Open your heart and take time out for God. Know this, that nothing

is more important than God in your daily life. When you put God first, God puts you first.

10   God is not only in the church, temple, and mosque. God is everywhere, in atoms, creatures and in the heart. When you turn your total awareness within, his presence is felt there. Whoever reaches God, is enlightened and liberated from this material world and suffering.

11   A smile creates happiness, for yourself and others and it costs us nothing. Why not become a smile millionaire. We all smile in the same light, which comes from our hearts. Smile even in the midst of sadness and darkness.

12   When you have good intentions to help others, the universal powers and people from all paths of life come to help you achieve your goals and you feel a deep satisfaction in your heart when the task is done.

13   Start your day with a little prayer and keep your consciousness high during the day. Before going to sleep, think and realize what you did wrong today so you do not repeat the same mistake again. Make a reminder to yourself such as tying a knot in a rope or writing it in your personal diary.

14   Usually people start their day with coffee or tea (Caffeine), fill their stomach with meat, cheese, and fried food and celebrate evenings with alcohol and smoke. Ask yourself, why am I poisoning my body? Do I want to be sick and die early, or do I want to live happy and healthy.

15   When you are deeply in love with someone, your mind is diverted from everything to your friend. Your mind becomes timeless in love, and you have no negative thoughts except sweet thoughts and good feelings in your mind. You begin to feel the flow of love energy and that is the energy of God. Love is the source to reach and experience God.

16   Anger is the reflection of self that is within. Be aware of your anger and the cause of your anger. Remove cluttered thoughts from your distorted mind. Think and see often from a different angle and everything will change. We make friends and enemies by the way we treat others.

17   Do not focus on others. Focus on your weakness. When you improve your weakness, it becomes your additional strength and you no longer feel a sense of inferiority in front of others.

18   Discipline is the key of success to life. Nature moves in order. The birds sing before sunrise and before sunset everyday. We tend to move against nature and stay away from nature, which causes stress, disharmony, imbalance, and disease. If you want to be happy and a successful person, be disciplined in your routines and activities.

19   The whole world moves in circles. Everything can be holy, if you remove your false beliefs, judgments, and

negative perceptions and see things in a neutral way with a healthy mind.

20   When you are introverted the whole universe and God is with you. If you are extroverted, you move away from your center and run after material goals. The more you run after material success and pleasures, the farther away you are from your higher self and God.

21   Do not give up even if you have failures. Success is always behind failure. Humayun was a Muslim emperor, who invaded India six times and was always defeated. In the sixth battle, he escaped and took shelter in a cave. He decided to give up. At that time, he saw a spider, which was climbing up and fell down 6 times, but the spider did not give up and succeeded in the seventh attempt. This gave him an insight and confidence and he succeeded in the war in his seventh invasion of India.

22   Love and sex are two different things, like the sun and the moon. The place of sex is in the mind and the place of love

is in the heart. Love means surrender of self and death of ego. Love binds people together and creates oneness of the two souls.

23   The light of the Lord shines in those who have God consciousness. Sing the glory of God, care for humans and animals, and share the words and teachings of God and love each other. Those who have God consciousness are far away from worries, fears, guilt and depression and they are protected in all aspects of life.

24   You do not need to read books, magazines or scripture to know and understand the meaning of love. Love is the beautiful energy of God, which is only felt in the heart. Even animals and those who are blind can feel it.

25   The universe is our strength. When human minds work together, they create beauty, love, peace, and harmony and strength in the environment. When bad political or fanatic religious leaders divide them for their own selfish purposes, the powers are scattered and the wise suffer. The

foolish get enjoyment by dividing people and ruling over others.

26   Do not hurt others as it adds more sufferings to the people and the world. Forgive those who have hurt your feelings in the past and leave everything to nature and God. The universal law is that each negative action has a reaction and sometimes it returns right away with a heavy force. Learn to live simply and peacefully and give life to others. The solution for all emotional problems is love, kindness, and forgiveness.

27   A real hero is one who does good things beyond his limits, sacrifices everything including job, money, time, and possessions to help others and to serve the lives of others.

28   Do not disclose the secrets of your life to a new friend or strangers. If the friendship breaks up, they can use the secrets or your weakness like weapons against you.

29   God never discriminates against one person or religion while favoring another person or religion. Only those who have lower level consciousness and higher ego would do that. Remember the power never stays at one place or with one person. It shifts like the sand in the desert.

30   The way termites eat the wood slowly; so it is the way in which stress affects mental health, which in turn slowly affects the body. Beat the stress by positive thinking, being organized, doing things carefully and patiently, maintaining a sense of humor, having a balanced diet, changing your life style, maintaining proper sleep and exercise.

31   If you go all around the world, you will be surprised to see that human behavior is the same in terms of sleeping, eating, talking, and mating. What makes you different among all human beings is your personality, intelligence, good attitude, good actions, and good deeds for mankind.

Inner reflections

FEBRUARY

1   Do not be scared of change. Nothing is permanent in this universe. The only constant thing is change. We all get accustomed to living with things, people and places and avoid change. Sometimes, change may be good. Remember whatever happens, it is for the best. Even when bad things happen, we can be reminded that good things will come to us later in life.

2   We all come empty handed to this world and when we leave, we leave the same way. What stays with us is our good karma, which has been recorded in our soul and the universe.

3   The things you have to do tomorrow, do them today and the things that you have to do today, do them now. Otherwise the work will be pile up, and you will be more frustrated, which can cause mistakes and accidents.

4   Life is full of joy, happiness, sadness and suffering. The strongest person is one

who remains the same between joy and sorrows.

5   Sometimes you ask why am I sad and others are hapThat is because of your choices and actions in the past, which are affecting you in the present. Increase awareness, think wisely, and make better decisions for your present and your future. The wise person is one who makes mistakes, learns something from them and corrects them. But the foolish person keeps making the same mistakes and causes more suffering for self, family, and friends.

6   Honesty is the best policy. When you do something wrong, admit it. To cover a lie you will have to speak a hundred more lies, then it will become your habit. One day you will realize that you are in trouble and you will ask people for help. They will never come to help you if they believe that you are lying again. People forgive you when you admit the wrongdoing and apologize for your bad actions.

7   Do not feel lonely when you go through separation, rejection, loss, divorce, and death of a loved one, accident or sickness. Be strong in life. The gold cannot shine until it passes through intense fire. Sometimes God tests our faith, patience, and will power. So be like the gold and understand that each suffering is making you stronger and bringing you more closely to God.

8   Physical needs are natural but the desires are the projection of your mind. The more you seek God; you achieve peace of mind and deep satisfaction in your heart, and all the desires for worldly things end.

9   Our thoughts move constantly like the waves move on the ocean. Our thoughts do not stop even during sleep. The only time our thoughts stop is when we control our breath and are in deep meditation. The act of introspection is not being an intelligent observer but a feeler.

10   The modernization of civilization and achievement in industry has created convenience, but they have also caused

pollution, disease, and an unnatural environment. When you lose touch with nature, it results in sorrow because you cannot enjoy God's beauty. Plant a tree in your house or in the neighborhood. Watch it grow and feel the nature around you.

11   Your real self is layered like an onion. During childhood we are free and natural but as we grow old, we are conditioned by parents, others, and society. The real self is suppressed and you act or behave the way people or society want. If you want to rediscover your real self then go away from the crowded city to a forest or a mountain and meditate on your breath and nature. You will drop back to your center, which leads to enlightenment.

12   When money is lost some material is lost, when anger is lost, a relationship and a friend is lost, but when character is lost, everything is lost.

13   A good family is one, which stays together, works together, plays together, and prays together.

14   When it comes to a survival situation, pray to God to help meet your basic needs. When you call to God with a pure heart, he/She comes to look after his/Her children like a mother comes to soothe her child when they cry or are in discomfort/danger.

15   Necessity is the mother of invention. No one knows who invented fire and the concept of the kitchen. It is believed that before civilization there was a fire in the jungle and the hungry people found the dead animals in the fire. When they ate roasted birds and animals, their taste led to the discovery of fire and cooking. You should also invent things in the world, like a child, who is always curious to learn the function of everything.

16   A man's biggest weakness is his denial that he needs to change his habits or that he has certain problems that need to be addressed. If you refuse to listen and ignore the suggestions from others, you will be at the same place as where you were several years ago and you will be the same person when you grow old.

17   Each day and every moment is very precious. Do not waste your time gossiping, criticizing or cheating others or observing what they are doing. Make the best out of every situation or day if you can, as life is very short. If you have done good deeds/karmas and have accumulated lots of blessing, you will not feel sorry when you leave this world.

18   A charity done with good intention to help others is equal to ten trips to church with pilgrims.

19   Marriage is the biggest adjustment of our life. The foundations of marriage are: love, respect, trust, honesty, caring, and support.

20   Eating is a joyful activity. Food nourishes our body, mind, and soul. Do not crave for tasty or spicy food. Crave for healthy food as our thoughts and emotions are directly affected by the food we choose and the way we eat. God gave us 32 beautiful teeth. Eat, chew, and bite your food at least 16 times as this increases

concentration, patience, and aids in digestion.

21 The whole world revolves around money. The love of money is the root of all evil. It divides friends, families, societies and nations. Do not be jealous if some one is richer than you. Be satisfied with what you have whether it is a little or a lot. Money can buy material possessions but money cannot buy love, happiness, health and friendship. People have interviewed the richest people of the world about money and happiness. They said that they have everything, but do not have peace and happiness. This indicates that money is not the answer to everything only love truly moves the world.

22 Do your work without expectation of attention, praise, and reward. A work done with good attention, intention, and commitment brings good results.

23 Do not try to change others. If you have the same habit or problem, first try to control your own habit or problem. If you can change for the better, then you can be

a good role model for others. When you change, the whole world changes.

24   Our body is like a chariot. Our mind is the controller and our five senses are similar to five horses of the chariot. One who knows the power of their soul knows the art to controlling their mind and senses. You too can learn self-control and guide the horses in the right direction towards God.

25   The best strategy to becoming productive is to think and plan out the project, then coordinate with others and take appropriate actions to achieve desires and feelings. Always maintain self-confidence and faith in God when taking actions then the outcome will be fulfilling and productive.

26   We make friends and enemies depending on the way we speak, act, or behave towards others. We must always think before we speak or act. Bad words and swearing hurt the emotions and feelings like piercing bullets.

27   If you want your wishes to come true,
      then make a list of your wishes. Present
      one wish a day to the first bright star that
      appears in the sky after sunset or to a
      morning star or any moving light that
      you see in the night sky.

28   Out of control attachment is the cause of
      misery, pain and suffering. Do not be over
      attached to people and places because
      when you detach yourself it causes pain
      to everyone.

Inner reflections

MARCH

1   Do not make any major decision when you become upset or angry with someone as your consciousness and intelligence drop into lower chakras (energy wheels in the body). In this state of mind, you may not be receptive to ideas, suggestions, or counseling. You just want to blow out everything. When this happens, take three deep breaths, drink some water, and remove yourself from the immediate environment. Then spend your energy doing a constructive activity or ask God for help and peace.

2   Do not mistreat or judge someone who belongs to a particular group, race, nation or if he/she is poor or helpless. We are the children of the same Father who loves all his children equally.

3   A real leader is one who has courage to confront his enemies, voicing displeasure against their wrong actions and policies. At the same time, a real leader inspires

mankind and cares for their happiness, needs and safety.

4   Do not be frightened of death, as death is life also. The way we throw or give away our old clothes and acquire new clothes, this is the way a soul leaves one body and enters into a new body. Souls never die, souls are immortal. Remove the fear of death from your mind and live a full and happy life.

5   Whenever you accomplish something, thank God and the people who supported you to reach that state in life. Do not fuel your ego by thinking that I am smart, I am powerful etc. Learn from nature. Trees give shade, shelter, fruit, flowers, and nourishment to us and water gives life to all. In the same way, the more you grow or become rich or powerful the more humble and helpful you are to others.

6   Never generalize your ideas about a culture based on a bad experience. You may be wrong in your judgment as each person from one family or culture

behaves differently. In the same way we have five fingers on our hand, they have similarities but function differently.

7   Whenever you read, type, or watch something on TV, it puts pressure on the nerves, of your eyes and mind. Blinking your eyes rests the eye muscles, nerves and mind. Eyes are the window of the soul and a precious part of the human body. Always keep them clean and rested.

8   Blessed is the one who maintains a strong faith in God, not only during joyful times but also during sorrows. Blessed are those who find God's love in doing things together and who also thank God for all things that happen positive and negative.

9   Peace and harmony start from our mind and spread throughout our environment and reaches to our neighbors, societies, and nations. If peace and harmony are disrupted, it results in pain and suffering for the people of the world.

10   Everyone goes through the process of aging. Whatever God and nature gives us at birth, gets taken back from us in old age. Our body becomes weak, memory declines, and our hair turns gray; our teeth fall out, and our vision and hearing also decline. Are these not enough witnesses that in life we should do something meaningful in our youth?

11   Imagination is more powerful than experience and knowledge. Imagination is a powerful tool to search, observe, and discover things within your own body, mind, and environment. Imagine and explore your inner powers and use them to reach your destiny, like a child who builds towering castles through his/her imagination.

12   Joys and sorrows are the two sides of the same coin. Do not feel bad or lose hope if you have many sorrows. Remember, after each sunset there is a sunrise next morning. The lotus flower grows in mud but still blossoms above the mud.

13   When you stand to protect the rights of others and their safe future, God stands right behind you to give you great success in your mission and deeds as well as satisfaction in your heart.

14   Knowledge is not something, which should be kept in a secure place in your mind. The more you give it away the more it multiplies, and the more it will continue to help others now and in the future.

15   Never stop learning even when you grow old. This is a special time to learn those things which you never had time to learn before. The more you learn and enjoy, the more you cherish life and its meaning.

16   Man can be worse than an animal if he is not taught morality and encouraged to follow the rules of family culture, society, and government. What separates man from animals are intelligence, spirituality, family, and social values.

17   Life is incomplete without love. Love never demands, punishes, resists, or divides others. Love expresses inner feelings, experiences the energy of God, heals emotions, and unites people.

18   Man and God have been fellow travelers since eternity. Both are lovers full of divinity.

19   The human mind has two sides, one kind and the other cruel. No one is born as a criminal or murderer. It is our choices in the midst of life's circumstances that lead us to be cruel and break the law.

20   The success of a man or a nation cannot be superior unless the foundations are based on love, respect, good principles, fair rules, high ideals, and unity.

21   The mind is the hardest thing to control. Always keep your mind occupied in good and constructive ways. An empty mind is like a devil's mind, which always looks to cause troubles for others.

22   No one is perfect. We may be an expert in one thing but may be inept in another. We learn through our mistakes, losses, and failures. Sometimes, when we have made bad decisions, it is because we have not asked God for help.

23   Do not rely on others or expect too much from others. When an expectation is created, and is not met, it gives emotional pain. Be independent and do things for yourself. This makes you grow strong and gives you pleasure and high self-esteem.

24   Patience is the key to all success in life. When you lose patience, you lose respect, and a good opportunity to achieve something meaningful.

25   Philosophy is thinking about the universe, nature, God's creations, reality and people and their behaviors, from a different angle and a higher point of view.

26   No religion is superior to any other religion. No religion teaches violence

towards others. It is the selfish religious leaders and politicians who divide people and rule the nations and the world. People will unite when fanatical leaders and corrupt politicians are moved out of religions, power, and politics.

27   Look upon all the animate beings as your friends, for in all of them there resides one soul.

28   Battle any negative thoughts in your mind (inner world) before it becomes reality. Be aware of your negative thoughts and replace them with positive thoughts. When your thoughts are changed, positive actions will follow.

29   The higher values we possess not only come through the family, society, or a nation but these values also come and are refined from inner experience and higher consciousness.

30   The world cannot continue without men and women, God created both. Together they make love, unity, and prosperity, and

also create harmony. Life is incomplete without one, they both create the whole.

31   It does not matter whether you do a small or a big favor for someone. It is the intention and act of kindness, which helps someone in difficulty. They will always thank you now and in the future, and when you are in trouble or have difficulty, they will be the first to come and help you in a difficult time or in a difficult situation.

Inner reflections

APRIL

1   The human being, endowed with intelligence and discriminating power, is his own teacher. Through direct observations and inference he guides his well being.

2   The self-controlled man should not move away from his path even when attacked by other people under the sway of primitive tendencies.

3   The size of the moon changes but the moon does not, similarly the state of mind changes but not the spirit.

4   No one can live without breath. Breath is life. It is a bridge between the body and the universe. Each incoming breath is life and each outgoing breath is death. The enlightenment lies between the pauses of two breaths. One who can learn the art of control can follow and feel one's breath and in the gaps can achieve heavenly experience and improve emotions, health, and life.

5   Do not waste your hard earned money on the lottery, gambling, stocks, drugs, alcohol, and prostitution. These habits lead to health problems, bankruptcy, and will ruin your family, career, and social life. Save your money for rainy days, the education of your children, travel, charity, and retirement. Be wise when spending or investing your money.

6   People go on talking about love but they never love. Love is something which cannot be learned watching others, reading books, watching movies, or browsing through entertainment magazines. Love is an eternal experience, which creates vibration in your heart, imagination in your mind, and a special light in your eyes.

7   Our mind has the capacity to store billions of thoughts in our memory banks. The more full it is, the more tension there is. You cannot learn to meditate unless you empty your mind. Clean one chamber in your mind everyday. Within a week you will begin to feel light, happy and centered.

8   Parents, schools, universities, teachers, and doctors always focus to train their minds but there is no one who focuses to train the heart except spiritual masters, priests, and others who wholeheartedly study the scriptures and religions.

9   A man is like a hard rock but when he falls in love he becomes soft like a flower. Absence of love is the cause of hate, disharmony, arguments, maladjustment, emotional problems, and wars.

10   Jesus said, if those who lead you say to you: Behold! The kingdom is in heaven; the birds of heaven will precede you! If they say to you that it is in the sea, then the fish will precede you! But the kingdom is within you and the kingdom is outside of you.

11   Lust is a black cloud; it conceals the light of the soul and the power of discrimination, which further covers reasoning power, and knowledge. When lust leads the senses, mind, and reason, man goes swiftly down the path of decline.

12   The man who is full of faith obtains wisdom, he has mastery over his senses, and he goes swiftly to supreme peace.

13   A karma (action) becomes a cause leading to another karma (action), which has its effect, and so is created by actions, which take us through births and deaths. But it is not karma (action) in itself, which creates the chain of causation. The chain is really created by false love and hatred.

14   Constant striving of knowledge for the spirit, direct intuition for the purpose of knowing truth, this is declared to be true knowledge (wisdom). All against this is ignorance.

15   God is the light of all lights. Him they declare to be beyond darkness. He is wisdom, to be reached by wisdom. He is seated in the hearts of all.

16   Eat fresh and healthy food. Man is what he eats, says a German proverb. Mind is a product of the food you eat. So choose good places to shop, and eat food cooked

by one whose intentions are pure, the food is not fried, fattening or spicy, and the atmosphere around is peaceful. Do not eat in the midst of noise or with people who dislike you.

17   The Spiritual people focus on austerity and simplicity in life. Passionate people enjoy wealth, comforts, sense, pleasure, fame, honor, and respect; and the ignorant people aim to harm others and live in the darkness.

18   Like a lighthouse guides others to reach a safe harbor, in the same way a guru/master guides others to move away from ignorance to the path of god realizations.

19   Excessive work, deadlines to finish projects, lack of money, lack of sleep, and environmental stresses disturb and affect our peace of mind. These things create stress in our life. Stress weakens our ability to concentrate and affects our immune system, which further affects our organs and the body. In order to reduce the stress of the mind, reduce the stress

of the body through relaxation, exercise, good sleep, and massage, and then reduce the stress of mind through prayer, positive affirmation, and meditation.

20   Time seems to move slowly in mundane tasks. But when you put your whole mind into a constructive task, the time flies and you feel happy, energetic, and contented.

21   Violence has its root in jealousy, hatred and anger. Once it is acted upon, it leads to aggression and the spilling of blood in the immediate environment, whether in the family, society, or nation. Using love and creating unity binds people and removes anger, hate, and violence.

22   It is not important to live in a rich society with high standards. It is more important to live with your ideals, morals, and values, good virtues, and cultural freedom.

23   False perceptions and misunderstanding can be removed by confrontation and clarification of a particular dialogue

directly or through a mediator. Understanding and good communication are the keys to resolving personal and social problems.

24   Do not go too far or too deep in the ocean, as you may risk your life. In same way do not make choices and decisions, which can create financial problems or may affect your relationship with family and others in your peaceful life.

25   The best and the simplest way to remain calm, happy and healthy is to remind yourself to take ten deep breaths every two hours and say, I am bringing pure, fresh energy by breathing in, and by breathing out I am removing negative thoughts, anxieties, fears and toxins from my mind and body.

26   When you experience the presence of God in nature, in all creatures, in all human beings, and within yourself, you enter eternal life and touch the kingdom of God.

27   Our mind is very mysterious, one minute it wants one thing, and the next minute it demands something else. Sometimes it starts one thing, leaves it uncompleted, and then begins another thing. It always jumps like a monkey from one place to another place. It has lots of hidden powers and it can store a billion bits of information and can create very beautiful things if it is understood and controlled. If you know how the mind works, and know what is hidden in your mind, you can solve the mysteries of life and the universe.

28   Always do your work like meditation and become more sincere about self, others, work, life, and existence. Great results and rewards will manifest themselves in all aspects of your life and you will become a special person that people will look upon with great respect.

29   We all have a purpose in this life. One, who knows the meaning of life and sacrifices his life to help mankind, receives a higher status in the world. When this person dies, the whole world

cries, but the person smiles and gets a special place in heaven.

30   It is not a bad idea to have some good hobbies instead of bad habits. Hobbies divert your mind to accumulate beautiful things like collecting stamps, coins, books, jewelry etc. Also doing meaningful work like painting, gardening, and sewing, awaken the creative spirit. These things become a treasure and keep you busy and happy in life.

Inner reflections

MAY

1   The words of wisdom that inspire or create an insight within you are more important than any other material things, which only provide a temporary joy.

2   You cannot change others and the changes in your life. It all depends how you react, how you respond, how you cope, how you accept, and how you adjust with people and change of life.

3   Mahatma Gandhi's seven sins:
1.   Wealth without work
2.   Pleasure without conscience
3.   Knowledge without character
4.   Commerce without morality
5.   Science without humanity
6.   Worship without sacrifice
7.   Politics without principal

4   Do not fear death, as death also is life. We fear death, because we want to continue our attachment to sensual and worldly pleasures. If you have done enough good deeds you should have no fear of death.

You should welcome death to take you back to the eternal world.

5   Without courage you cannot win anything in life. Courage does not mean using impressive language or showing power and intimidating someone. Courage means having the self-confidence to face challenges, to be strong enough fight for someone's rights and life.

6   The world is one large university, where everyone is both teacher and student, learning different lessons of life. One day a student becomes a doctor, engineer, journalist, scientist, or businessman etc., and shares his/her knowledge and experience with others. The fact is that sometimes you are a teacher to others and sometimes you are a student learning from others.

7   True joy is not when you wish for something and you get it. True joy is an inner experience of the soul and it is felt when you experience true love.

8 Love is beautiful but when it is possessed for personal gain or power it becomes ugly.

9 It does not matter how beautiful, handsome, intelligent, rich or powerful you are? Your attitude is what matters. The Moon and Sun are beautiful but during an eclipse, this beauty is hidden and no longer appreciated.

10 If you want God to listen to your prayers and wishes, ask for only one thing at a time with a pure heart in the universe.

11 Committing a bad act is not only a crime and sinful but even having a single bad thought to harm or kill is a sin as well.

12 If you want to know about the best way to solve a problem, know thyself. All universal powers, beauty, and God are within. Do not search for them outside, search and feel and enjoy them inside.

13 When you are in a position of power, you want people to follow your commands

and not to ask questions. This intimidates and creates inferiority among people. Do not misuse or abuse your power. Keep the people around you happy and they will be more loyal and productive. No one is superior or inferior. Your first identity is that you are a human being and beautiful creation of God.

14   It is very easy to plant a seed of hatred in ones mind or in the mind of others. But it is very hard to remove the root of this plant when it sprouts and grows out of control.

15   Always be gentle to others. Be firm and fight only when you see someone is abusing or bringing harm to a child, woman, an elderly person, or an unarmed person, or when you are in danger. Otherwise live happily in peace and likewise let others live happily in peace.

16   Do not complain about misery and suffering to everyone, for the more you complain, the more it multiplies in your mind and ruins your peace of mind. Express your pain and suffering to the

right people, follow their advice, act accordingly and then forgive and move on.

17   Life is divided into phases, childhood, adulthood, and old age. The foundation of childhood relies on your parent's direction and your environment. The foundation of adulthood rests on your development in childhood and your association with others. The foundation of old age relies on your deeds in adulthood.

18   You do not own this body. God has lent it to you. Do not make it impure through improper use of your senses, and bad habits. If you don't keep it pure and clean, you will be very guilty when you are called back and asked about your karmas on earth.

19   You are what you believe. Your belief plays an important role in life influencing whether you will be a success or failure. Remove all the false beliefs in your mind. Believe primarily what you see, hear, or experience, not what you heard from others in your childhood.

20   When you make wrong decisions and wrong choices, no one can relieve you from your suffering. You have to pay the price for your mistakes and go through suffering until you realize what is best. Visualize and correct your mistakes and make better decisions now and for the future.

21   There are times when you feel like there is nothing to do and you feel bored. In fact, this is the time to do those things, that you could never get started because of your busy life style.

22   Make an appointment with God. You always complain you don't have enough time for prayer and meditation but you always have time to gossip, time to roam around, time to sleep and time to meet others. If this is you, then your life is useless. Set aside 10 minutes a day to talk with God. Remember that God is more precious than diamonds and pearls.

23   The greatest quest of human life is to know who you are, where you are, and how you are different from others? Once

you have God consciousness and realize the purpose of life, you have all the answers.

24   People think of God only when they go through sorrow or suffering. If they think of God all the time then there will be no sorrow or suffering.

25   If you are honest, intelligent, and brave then no one can point a finger at you. Stand tall and reflect on what is right and good.

26   Do not pursue desires for earthly wealth, material possessions, and power. Desires are born out of the mind. The mind always wants to grab more things one after other, and is never satisfied, just like a child who has many toys but still wants another new toy. Know the inner core of your being and listen to your heart and pursue only those dreams and goals, which are good and real and bring real joy, happiness, success and satisfaction in your life.

27   Stress and tension lead to mental disorder and disease. The stress comes when we live or work in a conditional environment, when we make wrong choices, or we are forced by external forces to follow the rules or meet a deadline at work. It takes only a minute to breathe in and out slowly to release the mental tension and confusion from the mind. The peace felt by a heart can transform peace in the tense mind. A rested mind can imagine and visualize things better than the tense, disturbed, and agitated mind.

28   A person cannot see his/her face in a mirror, which is covered by layers of dust. Similarly, one cannot see or feel God unless the mind is cleaned and there is purity in the heart.

29   A wise person avoids anger because it disturbs peace of mind and hinders spiritual progress. It is wise to observe and remain silent when angry and forgive the other person for their misbehavior. Anger begins with emotions, ego, and ignorance and always ends in violence, destruction, and repentance. Think first

before you speak, act, or make a major decision. "You are the architect of your joy and sorrow".

30   Truth is higher than everything else; but it becomes higher far when you are living by truth and not living your life in dualism.

31   When a service is done out of love for others, it creates a solid bond and a close relationship between two individuals. But when a service is done to gain something in return, it creates a conditional relationship. This type of relationship can be shaken or broken by small disagreement, a different opinion, an argument, or misunderstanding of communication and actions.

Inner reflections

JUNE

1 You may be a very spiritual person but if you do not love God and the people around you, all the spiritual practices become useless and you still live in darkness.

2 The way two swords or two guns cannot be placed in one case, in the same way love and hate cannot dwell together. If you follow the path of love, all the hatred, fear and sorrow will vanish.

3 O God! People ask you to give them money, jobs, pleasures, companions, houses and children but I ask for your love, devotion, and blessing.

4 When you are in love, you forget about yourself and sacrifice everything, and that sacrifice is gracious and makes love even stronger.

5 If you ask a beggar to give you lots of money, he may not be able to give you anything. In the same way, if you ask

someone to love you and if they are self-centered and have never loved another, how can they love you?

6   There are three types of people:
1. The first type of person will respond to correction, make changes and never make the same mistake again.
2. The second type of person continues to make the same mistake again and again even though constantly corrected and reminded.
3. The third type of person, doesn't care, won't listen to anyone and will never change.

7   God's love is always pure and unconditional, but human love is often conditional and has desires to fulfill needs.

8   A true Karma yogi is one who remains in this world but remains unaffected by it's objects, people, and distractions.

9   Your shadow always follows you. In the same way, your good and bad karmas are

recorded in your subconscious mind by the universe and follow you from death to heaven.

10   You have only 8 hours a day to accomplish your short-term goals. Think about how you can do your best and how you can benefit after you accomplish them? Be patient. If you have not accomplished something within the same day, do not worry. You can finish it tomorrow.

11   Do not retaliate even when people insult, criticize, reject, or harm you. Let go of that experience and emotion, maintain your calmness and peace and leave everything to God. He will create a better lesson for them.

12   Sometimes too much knowledge can be harmful. As you begin to question and rationalize your way, you lose touch with reality. No special knowledge is needed to know love and God.

13   If you really want to be successful, first set realistic goals, and strive hard to

accomplish them. Your vision, insight, self-confidence, skills, knowledge and experience are the tools you need to accomplish your goals easily.

14 A radio cannot broadcast the music clearly until you tune it and get rid of the static. In the same way, our minds cannot think clearly if they are full of negative thoughts and emotions.

15 Every experience in life teaches you learn something about people and the world. The wise person is one who learns from his/her mistakes. Reform yourself, and then there will be no barrier to success.

16 When you came into this world, the destiny of your life was set in the lines of your palms. Your parents, grandparents, and teachers shape your childhood. In adulthood you are the architect of your joy and sorrows, and you are the creator of your destiny.

17 If you cry for your losses or failures then you are like that child who cries whenever

his/her toy is broken or taken away. But if you cry for God, your tears will become pearls; your heart will be purified. When you become closer to God, your life is blessed.

18   On every birthday, or at the New Year, make a resolution to give up your bad habits, and take initiative to take steps to accomplish something creative in the New Year. Also it is wise to initiate fasting at least half a day on your birthday.

19   Each day spend 10 to 30 minutes in silence. Silence allows union with God. Only those who practice silence are able to hear God's whisper (intuitive messages), feel peace within, share love, and serve others selflessly.

20   Wise people do not interrupt while others are talking. They do not condemn, criticize, or speak harsh words. They listen carefully, understand fully, think wisely, and speak honestly. Deep wisdom lies in listening not speaking.

21   The past is history; the future is a mystery, so enjoy the gift of the present, which is real, not illusion.

22   You may have tasted every special food; you may have tried many things through your senses. Have you ever tried to meet and know a master or God?

23   A most beautiful experience is when you enjoy nature, appreciate others, do something meaningful for someone, feed a hungry person, meet another spiritual person, learn something, solve an old problem, improve your relationship with someone, pray for someone, give love to others, or help someone to relax and meditate so that they can release mental and physical tension or resolve an emotional problem.

24   We always complain about work and not having enough days for fun and vacation. Count out 365 days and then how many weekends, holidays, sick days, and vacation days that have been used; then realize how much time is devoted to work and how much more vacation that

is needed, use your time wisely and learn to live earnestly.

25 You do not lose anything in asking when you do not know or understand something. If you do not ask question or get some help, you will never find the answers and you will never learn anything.

26 One who is committed to his/her words, work, and family responsibilities, does not provide lip service, they makes things happen.

27 The wise man leads a simpler life without any complications. The unwise person always keeps adding activities and material possessions and repeating the old ways of doing things, thus keeping their life complicated.

28 Finishing ones education, finding a new job, starting a new business, finding the right life partner, saving money for rainy days, and buying a house are the most important decisions of everyone's life. Check and see how many wise decisions

you have made in these major areas of your life.

29   Today I am choosing to be happy, to be calm and patient in every situation, to be wise in all my creations and decisions, to be understanding in my expectations, to be responsible for all my actions, and contented with all my needs and possessions.

30   It matters little who your parents or ancestors are. It matters more what you become? What is your character? How do you make a stand for others? What do you do for others? How much blessing, love, and social support do you receive from others? This world only salutes those who sacrifice everything for humanity.

Inner reflections

JULY

1   If you are looking for the answers to your problems, increase your awareness of your immediate environment. You may find the answers when you see something, hear a song, read some old papers or books, talk to a friend or counselor, or you can ask God to guide and help you.

2   God does not want us to only work, work, and work. That life is meaningless. God wants us to only Love! Love! Love! A life full of love and compassion for others is meaningful.

3   Seeing is believing. People do not believe until you show them. You need to prove yourself to people in two circumstances:

-    When you have done something wrong and you have promised to make a correction and improve.
-    You have discovered and gained something special, which is beyond the imagination of an ordinary

man, and you make it work, and people benefit from it.

4   The purpose of life is to realize that our body is mortal and changes are happening within and around us every second until life ends. But our soul is immortal which is not affected by any changes, temptations, and attachments.

5   Responding to people's attitudes, behaviors, and hatred sometimes results in over reaction, and this chain of over reaction continues until both sides come to an understanding and are able to compromise with each other. Remember that reaction-to-reaction is very dangerous. People always retaliate when they are in power. When you deal with a tough or dangerous person, use your soul consciousness, not ego consciousness.

6   Most people in the world, it seems, are moving, collecting or gaining more joy, power, money, comforts, land, and possessions; but there are only a few people who care about world peace.

7   The noblest person is one who has control of his/her desires, lust, greed, and hate; does not complain, tolerates everyone, and embraces everything that comes his/her way.

8   Our minds wander whenever we pray or meditate. Why not ask our mind to wander towards God rather than towards worldly things.

9   When you are upset, you make others upset or angry, and when you are happy, you make others happy. Choose what you want to be, happy or upset?

10   Contemplation means all your thoughts move in one direction. Concentration means focusing on a single thought or object, and attention means you see or hear only relevant things instead of everything.

11   God dwells in our hearts. The soul also dwells in our hearts. It moves to our eyes when we are awake, and moves to our throats when we talk and sing; moves to

our hands during help and healing, and moves back to our heart during sleep, and merges back to God when leaving the body.

12   The way you need to dial a number or type a password to be connected with someone, in the same way you need to recite a particular mantra to reach and communicate with God.

13   We live in an age of ignorance, hatred, and distress. If we attempt to increase spiritual awareness in our societies then there will be more love, peace, unity, kindness, charity, and prosperity in the world.

14   If you get hurt easily, then you are like a puddle of water that is easily disturbed when a small piece of stone is thrown into it. Be like a solid rock in the ocean, which is not affected by the power of the waves and remains unmoved.

15   Avoid falling into debt; because once you get into debt, it becomes very hard to

get out of it. Control your psychological needs and the habit to use charge cards frequently. Spend money within your income and budget. When you have no debt, you live happily and peacefully.

16   Replace negative thoughts with positive affirmations in your conscious and subconscious mind. I am calm, I am relaxed, I am happy, I am in the present, God is with me and around me, I am making good decisions etc.

17   The secret of a happy and successful life is higher intelligence, positive thinking, gratitude, and self-awareness, controlling your mind, emotions, and senses. Balance your daily routine and activities, organize your work, remain truthful, and have faith in God and work as a team with others.

18   Do not criticize others and do not listen to the criticism of others. These kinds of negative thoughts and negative energy make you think the same way as others who have negative perceptions of people and the world.

19   Do not steal or possess others property.
It s considered a sin. Always ask or get
permission from others to use their item/
money/land, returning them in good
condition then thank them for lending
their possessions to meet your needs and
goals.

20   You cannot become a spiritual person just
by going to church, being a vegetarian, or
reading some holy books or scriptures.
To become a spiritual person you must
purify your heart and confess your
bad karmas. Then search for a guru/
master to initiate and enlighten you to
move on the spiritual path. The guru/
master is a messenger of God who has
great knowledge about God, life and the
universe, and has the key to unlock the
hidden powers within you.

21   A guru/ master is one who is not attached
to people, money, and possessions. He
leads a simple life, he never gets angry,
remains quiet, shares love and knowledge
with others, maintains discipline in his
routines, rituals, and prayers, is totally

devoted to God and dedicated to serve mankind.

22   The true disciples of a guru/ master follow his teachings and follow the paths of love, truth, peace, self-realization, and non-violence.

23   Sometimes you pray to God but still bad things happen to you and you stop believing in God. These are the ups and downs of everyone's life. Based on your previous karma you experience pain and pleasure in the present. Do not test God or set conditions for love and answers to your prayers. No matter if you love or not, God still loves you, and you will see his miracles now and in the future.

24   When you become aware of super consciousness and use it positively you can take your mind to a higher spiritual plane or another place in the world. You can transmit messages to a person who lives thousands of miles away from you. You can predict future happenings, you can reduce or control the effects of evil and can change negative energy and bad

experiences in your life and in the lives of others.

25   Whenever you decide to do something wrong, immediately a second thought arises in your mind and tells you not to act. That is your super consciousness and the voice of God. If you do not listen the whisper of the infinite God becomes quiet and lets you do whatever you want to do, but later you realize that you should not have done the act. If you become aware and listen to your inner voice you are always happy and protected from doing what is wrong.

26   Yoga means union with God, discipline in daily routines and non-violence. Without doing yoga, the good current does not flow through our veins to our mind; and all meditation methods are incomplete without the knowledge and practice of yoga. Yoga is a first step to fitness and health, and meditation is the last step to connect your soul with the super soul (God).

27   Our mind has three faculties, Consciousness, Intellect and Ego. The person who uses more consciousness and intellect leads a peaceful and joyful life. On the other hand the person who always say "I", "mine", "me", his energy flows only in the lower level chakras (the energy wheels) below the navel area and he lives in the darkness (ignorance) and suffers according to his/her karma (actions).

28   It does not matter which God you believe in, Jesus, Allah, Ram, or Krishna. Remember that all the paths, religions, and teachings are different, but God is one and he loves all his children equally.

29   You may have seen some miracles in your life. Those people who have God realizations, do miracles and each of their action is done to ease the sufferings of others. When you have the same intention, realization, and good feelings to help others, then God's angels and cosmic powers will help you no matter where you are.

30   When you withdraw your attention and energy from several goals to one goal, success is more likely. Use your will power and self-determination to achieve your goals. First write your goals and objectives. Take small steps to accomplish your goals as each success leads to another success. Use your knowledge, imagination, and experience, and strive hard to achieve your goals.

31   Obsession is a repetition of a negative thought and compulsion is a repetitious action, which forms a particular habit. A bad habit can be changed to a good habit if you do not concentrate on negative thoughts. Redirect your mind, and replace negative thoughts with positive thoughts. Routinely concentrate on the positive to form new, healthy life giving habits.

Inner reflections

AUGUST

1   Health, intelligence, certain diseases, and anger come from genes and the environment. Thank God and your parents if you are happy, healthy, and an intelligent person. If you have low frustration tolerance and lots of anger, then release your resentments through prayer. Also, forgive others, along with your parents and ancestors. Look at their pictures, facing east for their wrong actions and negative qualities, which you may have inherited. Do a special prayer on your birthday until you feel a positive change in your emotions.

2   Do not make false promises to others. Be responsible when you make a promise to someone. If you cannot keep your promise for some reason, apologize to that person.

3   There are certain things, which cannot be accomplished alone. See what is good for humanity. A school, playground, hospital, a church or helping victims

of earthquake, hurricane or tsunami. Discuss human needs with friends and social or religious groups; encourage them and thank them for sharing ideas, food, clothes, medicine, equipment, land, and wealth for the benefit of others in need. The goal of helping others can be accomplished easily when you keep God in mind along with the people you are serving.

4   Children are the future of the family, society, and the nations. There is no substitute for real parents in the world. Invest time, love, care, and attention in your children and save money for their education. They will be grateful to you when they become adults. Parents and teachers shape the child and that child may shape a society, nation, or the world.

5   Make your home a workplace, for love, peace, compassion, and joy. Be loving and caring to your guests and kind to strangers. Whoever comes to your place, should not leave disappointed. Keep the doors of your house and workplace open

to all, especially to your neighbors, as they are the first ones to give you support and love during sickness, sadness, and times of crisis.

6   We all enjoy meeting new people and making friends. Do not judge others by the way they dress, talk, or how they respond to your questions, or what their living arrangements are like. People can become close and be your friend when they feel at peace, happy, and secure with your attitude and actions.

7   The easiest thing people give each other is advice. Sometimes, we do not know how to resolve our own problems, but most times we have good ideas and suggestions to help others. If you really want to help others, first help yourself and resolve your own problems. Make sure to have a right attitude when advising others. Do not give advice to someone until you are asked, as some people may be offended if you offer before they have asked for your counsel.

8   Wise people do not talk much or bring attention to themselves. They are quiet and attentive listeners. They use intelligence, not emotion when dealing with tough people. Their best qualities are simplicity, humility, generosity, kindness, strong character, soft speech, warm attitude, self-confidence, and strong faith in God.

9   The food you eat, purchased through your hard earned money, gives you deep satisfaction, joy to your mind and strength to your body. Food eaten by others, who have acquired it without doing any work or service or acquired through dishonesty or stealing, that food does not give real nourishment to the body, it causes laziness, creates guilt, insecurity, and inferiority.

10   When you rent or buy a new house, it looks very spacious. Slowly, you fill it with furniture and other household items, then it becomes full and not much empty space is left. In the same way, when you are a child your mind is blank. Whatever is written, observed, learned, or stored, it starts to become full and at

some point in life it starts to overflow like the water from a glass. So empty your inner storehouse; you have to clean your negative thoughts and resentments with visualization, positive affirmations and with an eraser of love, kindness, and understanding. Only then can you feel loved, full of light, joy and peace.

11   Never attempt to change yourself overnight. Write down your weakness, anxieties, fears, and bad habits on a piece of paper. You will be surprised to see how your mind has recorded and stored so many things you were unaware of, including repressed emotions. Now, set an action plan and start to work on one problem or emotion at a time, step by step. Measure your success by seeing the positive changes in your awareness, mood, actions, and good deeds in your daily life or by positive comments from others.

12   Pleasure, pain, and suffering come through the choices you have made in the past. Most of the time, you are left with a question about whether to

do something or not. If you become confused about making a good decision, then discuss this with a counselor, priest, your parents, your spouse, or a friend. If you are still confused about the decision, then you should pray to God to give you light, wisdom, and guidance so that you can make the right decision leading to positive changes in your life.

13   Do the work, which comes naturally to you. If the work you do and it does not suit your education, skills, temperament, and interest, it may cause disharmony and dissatisfaction, which further may affect your mental or physical health and relationships with coworkers and family. Choose work, which is fun, creative, challenging, productive, and provides you a monetary fulfillment for the time you invest in that work.

14   Knowledge is a gift of your personal attention, learning, experience, reading books and scriptures, and devotion to God. It is a treasure to share with others. The more you share, the more it increases and the more joy you will feel

in your heart. Blessed are those who use their knowledge to discover new things in nature and create inventions to help mankind. Love and nature are the parts of God, the deeper you go, the more you understand and feel them. God is right there.

15   A good teacher is one who is responsible, mature, and sincere. A good teacher knows what he or she is teaching and uses a gentle approach. But a great teacher is one who wants to give everything to all people and bring out the best in all of them.

16   Music comes from the divine, created in the mind, expressed through words, rhythm, and fingers, felt in the heart, and enjoyed by everyone. Most music, songs, and poems were created when people where going through happy times or through emotional turmoil. You do not need to know the language to enjoy the music. You just need to pay careful attention in that moment; respecting the musicians and appreciating their art of singing and instrumental creation.

17   Your life is incomplete if you have not studied about the lives of great masters, teachers, prophets, poets, geniuses, philosophers, scientists, leaders and humanitarians or read thought provoking scriptures. Once you read about them, you will be inspired by their creation, devotion, and sacrifice. You might learn something significant that will transform your life.

18   When men and women are not jealous of each other's status, positions, salary, possessions, and work, and coordinate things together, they create love, unity, harmony, productivity and prosperity.

19   Money is not real wealth. Health is real wealth. If health is lost, happiness is lost. Create a balance in different areas of your life, for example diet, sleep, sex, recreation, relaxation, and spirituality. Avoid smoking, eating junk food, drugs and alcohol, gambling and prostitution. Remember that higher awareness, self-control, and prevention are more important than cures.

20 Never take credit due others if they have contributed their time, talents, ideas, and efforts to obtain a goal. Always acknowledge others by mentioning their names in your work or by sending them a letter of appreciation. It boosts their morale and self-esteem for future efforts and productivity.

21 When you are attending a meeting, or addressing a group, act naturally while speaking. Make your first remark an affirming acknowledgement of the presence of the audience and make the second remark a good quote, which touches people's hearts and imagination. Make a pause in between sentences to let the thoughts drift into their minds, then continue your speech with examples from personal experience and continue to speak with confidence. Third, be aware of your subject and any time limits. End your speech by smiling and thanking the audience for listening and asking questions and making suggestions. Remember that the first impression is the best impression.

22   Most illnesses are caused when we ignore the needs of the body and constantly abuse it until we fall sick, develop psychosomatic symptoms, or contract a disease. Other causes can be hereditary or due to lack of nutrition, emotional indigestion, busy life style, lack of fresh oxygen, lack of exercise, lack of sleep and toxins in the body. Each illness should be treated accordingly, either it is medical or emotional.

23   Do not associate with friends who are consumed by bad habits, unhealthy activities, or crimes. The people you spend time with influence you, and you start to talk and act the same way. Choose to spend time with people who have good character and healthy habits and you will become a good and noble individual.

24   As nature is all around us, in the same way God's healing energy is around us. You just need to feel it silently by praying "O God, I need your healing energy to heal my physical illness or God give me your healing energy so I can allow it to flow to my family member who needs

healing". Visualize that person deep in your mind and feel the light or energy coming through the universe into your crown chakra (center of your head) and into your heart, going through your hands to the person you are visualizing. Then, send the energy or light back to the universe.

25   Every person has three parts of self and existence. One part is the real self (spirit), the second part is the ideal self (morals and character), and the third part is the external self (mind and matters).

26   Many things in our life can be reversed through money and support from others, however the cherished moments of childhood are hard to reverse unless you go back to your roots and create the same social situation with your family and friends again. Life is very short. Live your life fully everyday, for you never know what will happen tomorrow.

27   If a person is aware and responsible for their actions, respects the rules of society, helps to keep the environment clean,

shows respect and courtesy towards others, donates to the poor, helps others in emergencies and difficult situations, that person is one of the best citizens in the world.

28   The strength and civilization of a nation is measured by it's leaders, their integrity and character, high morals and values, fair tax laws, ethical policies, good social standards, safe living environment, freedom of speech, freedom for practicing religious activities, strong economic conditions, lack of corruption, higher education system, controlled population and pollution, modernization in agriculture, science, and technology and discipline and unity among its people.

29   Do not feel guilty if you have done something wrong. Apologize to others and confess your sins to God and start a new life. It is never too late to make changes in your life and take responsibility for your actions. Give up old ways and habits and replace them with goodness in your life.

30   Gandhi's desires and plans for mankind:
1.   To help others selflessly
2.   To unite human beings from all religions
3.   To use non-violence against injustice
4.   Helping poor and untouchables
5.   Practice spirituality
6.   Treat others with respect and love everyone
7.   Live a simple and peaceful life
8.   Practice honesty
9.   Focused goals in life

31   Geniuses are those who use their imagination and always do good deeds for others. Creative ideas lead to the development of helpful inventions and new positive ways of doing things. This creates a shift from the impossible to the possible.

Inner reflections

SEPTEMBER

1   Helping the poor, the helpless, being kind to children, helping parents in their old age, sharing love with others, are the acts of kindness and the greatest services to mankind and God.

2   Physical beauty changes as you go through the aging process but spiritual beauty blossoms if you have turned yourself inward and outward towards God.

3   Most unpleasant human behaviors occur due to jealousy, use of ego, misuse of power and religion, impatience, lack of money, self-centeredness, lack of attention, lack of sensory stimulation, or overriding desire to obtain tangibles in the material world. If you continuously want to seek these things, it means your mind is contaminated with greed, anxieties, anger, fear, frustrations, and sorrows.

4   Feeling lonely puts you in a lower state of consciousness, which affects your mind

and blocks positive thoughts and the flow of good energy. Believing and feeling that God is your companion and that he is always around you to guide, protect, and help you in all situations makes your faith more strong and increases love energy within you and around you.

5   Anything that causes envy can be stolen or destroyed by others. The character you have built up and the knowledge you have gained, good deeds you have done, no one can take those away from you.

6   When you begin to know and understand how your mind works, how you can control your mind and senses, ask who am I? What am I doing with my life? Where am I going? What is the ultimate goal of my life? When you begin seeking answers to these questions then you are moving in the right direction. God will give you good direction, trust in his love.

7   When all your attachments are to people, places and wealth, you experience sorrow, and your accomplishments are limited.

When your attachment is to God, there is infinite joy, peace, security, and more success in all paths of life.

8   Everyday can be a beautiful day and full of surprises and successes. It depends on what kind of thoughts you have in your mind. What you think, so you feel. Tell your mind, I am a gift of God and I will continue to give the gift of love to others.

9   Worries weaken the mind and heart. Worries can affect your mood, sleep, work, and performance. When you face tough people or face a stressful situation, you become more tense and nervous, which further affects the flow of energy, attention, ability to think clearly, and ability to respond to others. When others sense that you are nervous and shaky, they attempt to put you down. They win and you lose but if you calm your mind and consciousness, keep your emotions and senses in control, think positively, respond intelligently and call on God's name for help, your mind will become

powerful and you will be able to change others.

10   Seeing and feeling God's love is believing. Once you experience the nectar of God's name there will be no greater joy to experience in this world.

11   If you cannot learn to control the negative thoughts in your mind, then you cannot find peace no matter where you go, be it on vacation or on a retreat; these negative thoughts will still bother you until you really become aware of them and release them from your subconscious mind.

12   If you always look for praise and attention, you can be easily hurt when you do not get what you need from others. Living a life without expectations is simple and peaceful.

13   Breath is the most primitive sense and it is close to our being but God is closer to our being than our breath.

14   A work done with full attention, good thinking, and sincere effort brings beauty to the task and it won't need to be done again and there will be no regrets later. Always do your best and take pride in what you do.

15   Do not complain that others have wronged you. Look at the rose, it grows and blossoms among the thorns, but the petals are still soft, fresh, alive, and bring happiness to others.

16   Love is a pure feeling of the soul; it has nothing to do with physical bodies. It is a blissful state and being in love means being joyful.

17   Nothing is hard to achieve if you have made a firm commitment to achieve your goals. Concentrate your thoughts and energy on one goal at a time and success is more likely to happen.

18   When you give your heart to someone, you might get hurt and suffer heartbreak. When you give your heart and pray, or

chant a mantra with each breath, you will feel and experience the presence of God. You may suffer a broken heart but God brings healing.

19   Some people talk too much and laugh at others. They don't accept people as they are, nor do they accept criticism from others. Remember that energy and karma released is returned.

20   Think twice about your actions and their consequences. An action done without proper thinking, discussion, and coordination can cause failure, accident and ill will towards others.

21   Do not throw stones at the houses of others, as you also live in a house of glass. Live peacefully and let others live peacefully.

22   Life begins with your parents. Their love, care, attention, education, and protection nurtured your soul, your awareness, understanding, knowledge of the world, right choices, and right activities.

Continue what your parents began and you will find your destiny.

23   A relationship based on wealth, power, beauty, hopes, and expectation is similar to a child who makes a sand castle on the beach. It can be destroyed whenever there are waves of negative karmas. They touch and destroy the sand castle and the relationship in a moment.

24   It is very easy to find fault in others. People can even find faults in the best painting of the world. Do not focus on negative things, see good things in others and bring the best out of that person. Praise and reinforce hard work and right behaviors.

25   A light competition in the workplace can lead to greater effort and success. However, a cutthroat competition can be dangerous and everything might be lost when trying to defeat another person, which would lead to much regret.

26   When you continue your dishonest lifestyle, you will be caught sooner or later, and when you are caught and confronted and you lie, no one will believe you. Your integrity will no longer be taken seriously.

27   When someone blames, threatens, or becomes angry with you, be polite and respond appropriately. If the person escalates, do not argue, as a wise person is one who walks away from a troublemaker and looks for the right time and opportunity to explain things better and give them cause to question their behavior.

28   When everything goes well, it means that you have done something good. Do not fuel your ego; be proud of yourself in a way that makes things better and your life more simple because this is the only life you have.

29   You have tremendous magnetic powers – Love, knowledge, kindness, speech, and a smile. Use them wisely, you will attract everyone and you will become an

instrument of God. You can make good things happen in your life and the life of others.

30   Sometimes it is not what you say but how you say it that makes a big difference. People can misunderstand when you use emotions in your communication. People listen, understand, and appreciate it when you talk softly, make good points and lead by example. Do not lose hope when there are failures, disappointments, sorrows, or separations, from loved ones. Maintain a hope, keeping God in your mind and heart and good things will happen again. When one door closes, God will open another door for you. Hope is a beam of light in the darkness.

Inner reflections

OCTOBER

1   O lord give me your love and strength so I can touch the hearts of others and heal their bodies, minds, and spirits through words of wisdom, gentle and loving touch, and good deeds.

2   Sacrifice on behalf of humanity makes you a great person in the world. Mahatma Gandhi (great saint) sacrificed his life against discrimination and protested for the rights of black people in Africa. The reason he gave up his shirt that covered his upper body was because he saw a poor lady who did not have clothes to cover her upper body as she breast fed her child in public during winter. He gave his shirt to that lady to cover her body and said that it is not fair that she has no shirt to cover herself and her child while I, a man, have all the clothes I need to cover my body. Every sacrifice is glorious in life.

3   If you are really sincere in becoming a spiritual person and want to be connected

with God, then first connect yourself with the right people. Observe, listen, and learn good things from them. Then pray every morning before you start your day. Light a lamp or a candle and offer it in front of the picture of your guru/mentor then place it facing east or south. The lamp or the candle will remove the darkness and the negative energy from your living environment and it will cause the cosmic energies to enter to your place.

4   You do not need to tell God your excuses about not having enough time for worship. He knows you better than you know yourself. Just turn your total attention to God. He will give you tremendous power and will resolve your problems before you ask him to do anything. Through daily worship and meditation, you will be able to heal yourself and others.

5   As a mother does not ignore her child and run away when the child cries or the child is in danger, in the same way God loves all his children even when they do not love him. He helps those who call for help with a pure heart and pure feelings.

6   In the womb, a child is connected with his/her mother by the umbilical cord (gateway of life and energy). The child experiences the mother's breathing, thinking, sleeping, eating, talking, or walking. A child becomes a part of a mother's body, mind and soul. When the umbilical cord is cut after birth, the child is separated from the mother's body but another cosmic mother who supplies breaths to live and grow, connects them. If you visualize your belly button being connected with the universal divine mother, you will always be at the center of infinite peace, love, and divine light.

7   Every time you seek, worry, or work, you lose your mental energy. The mind gets tired and the body experiences the same. If you spend even 10% of the time you spend thinking about money, sex, power, and possessions, sitting in silence before God, your life will become problem free and you will gain more mental satisfaction even if you do little work or if you have little wealth.

8   It is good to chat in a group. It is good to learn meditation in a group but it is also wise to practice meditation alone or with your family, as their thinking of God and the purpose of meditation is the same. God dwells in those houses where he is invited with love, prayers, devotion, and meditation. If you can afford to make a small shrine area or room in your house then you do not have to go out to pray. God is in you, within you, around you, and God is in your home.

9   Life is full of mystery, the more you try to understand the depth of it, the more puzzled you become. Wise are the ones who go with the flow of life and accept whatever comes their way; even when discouraging things come they still accept them. Remember behind all dark clouds there is a golden lining. Increase your awareness of God every minute, day and night, then the mysteries will unfold and you will easily understand them and God will be in your smile.

10   The greatest enemies of the human mind are evil thoughts and anger. The

greatest enemies of the body are: toxins, impurities, hormonal imbalances, meat, alcohol, drugs, excess salt, excess sugar, pollution, and repressed emotions, all of which cause the disease. If you drink the nectar of the name of God, all the impurities will be washed away and a new life will begin within you and you will live a happy and healthy life.

11   Choose one good mantra or beautiful thought such as "I love you God, I love everyone, I have to share love and knowledge with others, I have to help others, etc. Maintain an awareness of that mantra throughout the day and before going to sleep each night. The good thoughts become powerful messages that unlock the infinite wisdom within allowing many infinite possibilities to come your way.

12   If you really want to clean the negative thoughts from your mind, then practice cleaning one chamber of your mind each time you wash dishes, do the laundry, or clean the house. You can also do this as you walk or pray.

13   This world is full of hypocrites; they live in ideas, make rules for others, keep money and power in their hands, and use others for the work that needs to be done. But they don't control the super powers. Only God controls the super powers. Our life and fortunes are dependant on the mercy and love of God. No matter what others do, be authentic and take action that encourages the best in others.

14   When we make efforts to create peace and spread the message of God, we do not need to speak our own words. God speaks through us and the one who listens becomes more wise. Those who listen carefully and follow the teachings, find joy, and improve their lives.

15   The energy of God is everywhere in the universe. The way we do certain things like operating a car and driving it, or the way we use a password to access a computer, in the same way we need to learn certain rituals and methods to open up the hidden cosmic energy (Kundalini) located in the base of the spine and to feel the powers of God. Then we will be able

to see and experience the magic of that crystal energy within us and around us.

16   Man and woman are at two opposite poles. Men are known for wisdom and strength and women are known for love, and care. They are imperfect without uniting their wisdom, strength, feelings of love and care. Once they give and receive true love, they experience the divine and become the whole of each other's incompleteness.

17   Do not work excessively. When you do things in moderation you lead a simple and peaceful life. Balance is the key to health, happiness, and success in life.

18   No matter how intelligent you are, when it is time to make major decisions in life you can still experience difficult situations. When that happens, always consult with an expert, a counselor, a priest, or experienced people in your community. If you do not find anyone, then simply consult with your higher self (inner guide) in silence and ask for

the best answers and solutions to your problems.

19 Our brain has two hemispheres and we have two ears, two eyes, two nostrils, two lungs, two kidneys, two hands, two legs, but we have only one heart. This means we can give our hearts (the supreme love) to only one person and to God.

20 You clean your body almost everyday, but ask yourself, how many times have I cleaned my mind? May be ten percent of the time in a year. We have more than 2 thoughts every second and about 50 thousands thoughts in one day and 50% of our thoughts are negative. Just think how many negative thoughts and emotions you have accumulated. If you spend only ten minutes each day before going to sleep, reviewing your daily thoughts, ideas and experience with others, you become more aware. Fifty percent of your negative thoughts and experiences will be enlightened. For the rest, you can use them as positive affirmations to clean your mind.

21   If you learn to control your senses, you can control your negative behavior. When you control your negative behavior, you make good choices. When you make good choices, opportunities come to you and you enjoy freedom. When you enjoy freedom, you no longer remain the slave of your mind, time, and worldly conditions. Do your best in your youth and enjoy your retirement.

22   We have a place to work and a house to live in. Do not mix up the two. When you leave work, leave everything there. Come home and relax, and refresh for the next day. Maintain cleanliness in your work and living environment. God's energy comes to those places and stays where people have purity of thought and cleanliness in their environment.

23   It is true that you can be a wealthy person. But you can be a spiritual person and draw closer to God. You just need encouragement and determination to detach yourself from the things of this world, to create an interest in spirituality. You do not have to be a scholar to know

and understand well, you just need to increase self-awareness and an awareness of God. You will seek God, and although you may not see him, you can sense his presence and miracles happening through you and around you.

24 If you see the beautiful creation of God, like mountains, trees, flowers, rainbows, stones, the sun and the moon, the ocean, birds, and the beautiful people around you; think deeply about these reflections of his beauty, and then think how beautiful he is.

25 Life is full of challenges. Whenever a project or problem comes to you and you do not know what to do or how to resolve it, instead of getting frustrated and upset, simply close your eyes and ask God for help. Break the problem into small pieces first and think where you need to start and where you need to end. Visualize and do all this mentally then write down these steps on a piece of paper and begin the task. If you are still not sure or confident, then see how other people have done the same type of work or project, then consult

with them. The more you do this mental exercise, the more you will sharpen your knowledge and skills.

26   The way one moon and one sun remove the darkness of the earth; in the same way one person can create changes in the lives of millions of people. Think of Jesus, Krishna, Rama, Allah, Guru Nanak, The Pope, mother Teresa, Gandhi and many other beautiful people who are spiritual masters, teachers, and humanitarians of the world.

27   No matter how busy you are in your daily work, keep thinking of God intently. Give time to yourself and your family and create time to serve others. Serving others is the same as serving God.

28   You always have a reason to accept people and situations or reject them. Use your wisdom to make a better decision. Do not be tempted by the possessions of others. If something is not going according to your nature and it appears everything is going wrong at work, immediately express yourself. If people do not cooperate or

listen to you, then express your concerns to the manager or an administrator. If you still see no change or progress then simply walk away from their environment.

29   When do you remember God; only on certain days and special occasions, or when things go wrong or you lose something or someone? Why not remember God everyday? If you remember him everyday, you will receive a special gift along with a beautiful expression of peace.

30   The way you have to study intently to obtain a degree or complete an education, in the same way, you have to meditate intently to meet God.

31   Keep a personal diary to track your spiritual progress; showing the time and efforts given for meditation, along with all the special things that happened to you each month. Review your progress at least annually and if you are going in a positive direction, smile and reward yourself. Write a poem, take a vacation, or go on pilgrimage. After that, your spirit will be lifted up ten times higher.

Inner reflections

NOVEMBER

1   Human energy is like electricity. Electricity is used in almost everything in our everyday lives. In the same way, human energy can take on different forms such as love, anger, and hate. Do not waste your energy by being angry or hating others. Use that energy to create harmony and to discover something meaningful for mankind.

2   It is human nature, whenever you are angry or upset with one person to transfer those feelings to another person. Be aware of your thoughts, emotions, and feelings. Think creatively, talk politely, act patiently and relate to people with kindness.

3   The way each drop of water fills a cup, in the same way, every penny saved builds wealth for days of misfortune. Always spend money within your limits. Do not borrow too much money from people and banks. It is easy to get money from them but it is very hard when you get into debt.

Simplify your life and be content with meeting your basic needs. True beauty lies in simplicity.

4   Every second you have two to three thoughts in your mind, which makes it very hard to concentrate. When you have to think deeply or focus on a certain project, your thoughts flow with each breath movement. The slower you breathe the fewer thoughts you will have. You will also have more peace, more energy and longer life. Be aware of your breath movement and slow it down from 16 times per minute to 8 times per minute, then you will learn to live in the present. When you are in the present, you are in touch with your being and God. This is the simplest method of meditation to connect your soul with the super soul (God).

5   When you do acts of kindness, you do the highest duty of human life. God is not impressed with wealth and other material objects. God favors acts of kindness, unconditional and pure love, and devotion.

6   The way a spider makes a web and then gets stuck inside and is unable to free itself, in the same way, we add lots of activities and material objects to our life and have only a little time for self, family, and God. If you really want to be free of this worldly web, think and act to untangle the knots and remove these layers of unnecessary things, which have made our life a puzzle. Live in the world but remain unattached to everyone and everything.

7   There are five major decisions of everyone's life:
1.   Getting the right education for the right job/business
2.   Finding the right life partner
3.   Buying a good home
4.   Raising children in a good and safe environment
5.   Saving enough money for retirement

8   Good thoughts nourish our mind and heart. Having a single thought to harm another is considered a sin. Always say

no to negative thoughts and say yes to "God".

9   Everyone and everything is important in life, however giving time to self, family, children, and God are the most important moments, actions, and deeds of life.

10   The whole universe is filled with vibrant cosmic energies. It is up to us to see, hear, touch, smell, and feel these energies. The way you turn on the light switch to have electricity in a room, in the same way, if you want to feel these energies, you have to go to special places such as the quiet of the mountain, the stillness of the forest, the rhythm of the ocean, and other quiet places to meditate. By doing this you will achieve tranquility in your mind and gain special powers to know and feel the universal energies and God.

11   A wise person is one who follows the advice of good people, uses awareness and good judgment, and learns from the mistakes of self and others, and never repeats the same mistake. An ordinary person, who does not think clearly, will

continue to repeat mistakes but eventually will learn from them, however a foolish person is ignorant and impulsive and will continue making mistakes and will never learn from them.

12   Our body has nine doors including five senses. The nose is the door to our consciousness. The most primitive sense is smell as everything flows through our breath movement including our thoughts, feelings, and emotions. Our breath takes us to the door of consciousness and helps us stay alive. Learning to control the breath, lowering the breath rate, and feeling the breath keeps us calm, relaxed, and healthy. Meditating on the heart through breath and the third eye takes us deep in the basement of our hearts where God resides.

13   The way a plant needs sun, air, water, fertilizer, and constant care to grow and stay green, in the same way human relationships need constant love, attention, care, trust, respect, good communication, and understanding to stay happy and healthy.

14   The secrets of a happy and healthy life are: pure and positive thoughts, a right attitude, higher awareness, good deeds for others, eating fresh fruits, vegetarian food, meditation, simplicity in lifestyle, stress free work environment, harmony in living environment, daily prayer, giving and receiving love, and getting social support.

15   Marriage is the greatest adjustment of everyone's life. Do not go after physical attraction, money, and possessions. Choose a right partner with a good temperament, common interests, and positive personality traits. See the beauty of the heart, not the beauty of the face, as the face can be deceiving leading to suffering, debt, violence, and divorce. Marriage requires acceptance of each other, respect for each other, nurturing each other through true love, and sacrificing unhealthy habits and lifestyle. Marriage is a union of two souls and two families.

16   No one is born evil in this world. It is the society and its social, political, and

religious leaders who create self-serving rules, sow the seeds of hatred, and divide man from man to fulfill their needs and do everything to stay in power. No religion teaches us to kill another human being or to commit suicide. God does not open the doors of heaven to those who have killed others for the sake of religion. God is not limited to one society, or nation, God is everywhere and in all human beings. Those who love others, help others, do good deeds for others, and receive the blessings of God. They lead a good life and experience a measure of heaven on earth.

17   Start your day with a little prayer and imagine white light and purple light surrounding you before you go out into the world to perform your duties. you will be filled with peace, power, and creative thoughts and you will be protected from evil. When you retire at night pray again and visualize your day and see if you have done anything wrong, then ask God to forgive you. Our subconscious mind becomes more powerful by using positive affirmations and prayer before

sleep to make a change in the next day and future happenings. Each day brings new hope to fulfill your dreams. Make the best out of each day.

18   Love energy always remains the same but it takes different forms with different people. No matter how far you live from your loved one or friends you can still feel their love in your heart and you can transmit your thoughts, love, energy, and healing to anyone through prayer and telepathy, even thousands of miles away.

19   The way you need a key to open a door, in the same you need a master or guru to initiate, bless, and to guide you to the path of light (wisdom). When you are tired of worldly experiences and attachment and you are ready to change, then your master will come in different forms and may appear even in your dreams. If you follow the advice of your master or recite a special mantra given by the master, you may unlock the hidden treasure within you and in the universe, and may achieve divine powers.

20   You are what you think and you are what you eat. Always think good, positive thoughts, choose healthy food, eat in silence, and eat slowly. Eat only when you are hungry. Do not eat when you are thirsty and do not drink when you are hungry. Take the amount of food, which can fit in two palms. Even a nectar becomes poison when it is taken in excess quantity. Eat food not only to satisfy your belly but also eat food, which gives nourishment to body, mind, and soul.

21   You are never too old to learn something new or to achieve a goal. Do not give up or be impatient. Make time to practice an activity with full attention and concentration. Focus and learn from trial and error and past mistakes, and continue to work hard. Remember that where there is a will, there is a way.

22   The world is like a large university. Learning brings knowledge, skill, and inner wealth and experience becomes our master. Never think that you know everything in this world. We learn from

each other. Someday you are the student and other days you are the master.

23   If you have moved on to a wrong path or you still choose to live in the past. Do not be angry or depressed. You always have a choice to make changes in your life. Never feel helpless and shy to seek help from others. Do not try to change others, when you change the world changes.

24   If you want to know the answers to your problems, simply learn to relax and visualize your life from past to present, be aware of your surroundings and attune yourself to nature. Use your faith and request God to be your guide to remove worries, fears, conflicts, obstacles, and problems. Remember when God is near, there is no fear.

25   There are many paths to reach God. The simplest ways to reach God are:
1.   True love
2.   Acts of kindness
3.   Prayers
4.   Chanting
5.   Meditation.

26 Whenever you achieve a state of self-realization and you give up your past, that is the beginning of a new life, full of higher awareness, joy, happiness, peace, knowledge, success, and prosperity.

27 The human mind is sometimes like a monkey's mind. The way a monkey jumps from one place to another place without any goal, it never completes one thing before starting to do something else. In the same way, the human mind wants to go here and there, do this and do that activity. This makes a person's mind more restless and dissatisfied. People who are successful, have control of their mind and do only one thing at a time. Their mind is fixed on the goal and a positive outcome.

28 One cannot be a real spiritual master, teacher, or a yogi without being freed from desires, sense gratification, material possessions, and material success.

29 It is not hard to become a friend of a tiger or snake, conquering a tough enemy in battle, going to the moon or Mars, learning

a different language, building a large tower or bridge, or riding a wild horse but it is very hard to sit still in meditation, controlling your own mind and being in touch with your own breath.

30 Who has God consciousness? One whose mind connects to God easily and finds more pleasure within doing human service. To such a person, happiness and sadness, heat and cold, honor and dishonor, success and failure, profit and loss are the same. They are not affected negatively by anything in this world.

Inner reflections

DECEMBER

1   Visualization is the most effective technique to see your past and future. Use your third eye, which is located in between your eyebrows. Find a quiet and serene place and sit or lie down on a bed or couch. Take three deep breaths to relax your mind, upper body, then the lower part of your body, then slow down your breath and feel the gap between your breaths. After this, bring your attention to your third eye, then choose the direction you want to go, to the past or to see things in the future. Make sure to start visualizing things from present to past or present to future. Be aware of emotions, weaknesses, and problems. Ask your higher self and God to guide you to eliminate the problems and give you the power to forgive those who have hurt your feelings or caused you sufferings in the past, and ask God to take you on the path of love and light.

2   We all have a purpose in this life. One of the major purposes of life is to be served by others and to serve others selflessly.

Serving others means serving God, and that should be the higher purpose of our life.

3   Everyone is born with unique qualities and these qualities are awakened through our parents and teachers, or when we come in contact with wise and spiritual masters who inspire us to think differently about life, religion, people, and God, and to do meaningful things in life. When we come to this point in life, that is the beginning of inner knowledge, which takes us to enlightenment and to our destiny.

4   You are the product of your childhood. Whatever you have seen, experienced and heard from others is stored in your subconscious mind. Whenever you go through a similar experience to what you experienced in the past, it will trigger the same belief or the same experience, and you will start to act or react to others and the environment. There is goodness in everyone. If someone has nine good qualities and one negative quality then you should not judge that person based on only one negative quality. You should

try to ignore the negative and focus on the good qualities of that person. This will bring out the best in that person, because within everyone there is a child and an angel of love and kindness, waiting and wanting to be released.

5   The basic, common principles among all religions are:
-      Love one another
-      Practice non-violence
-      Do not steal
-      Truthfulness
-      Do not commit adultery
-      Limit one's possessions
-      Honest dealing with others
-      Consciousness of God
-      God dwells in those places where love, food, and gifts are shared with the poor, sick, and the homeless; where people are cared for and where peace and harmony are practiced and maintained in society.

6   Knowing how all things and mankind function is called knowledge but knowing your higher self, seeing God in one

another, and experiencing God within is enlightenment.

7   The past is history and the future is mystery. Enjoy the present moment and make the best of it. Your future is based on the good decisions you make today. The seed of a plant is plain however it holds a beautiful plant within. When a seed is grown properly and it has been given expert care, it sprouts, blossoms, and looks beautiful for the future.

8   Each incoming breath gives you life and each out going breath removes the toxins, tension, and poisonous gases from our body and gives us continuous life. To heal your body, mind, and spirit, visualize your favorite color or white light with each incoming breath and visualize a gray or black color with each out going breath at least 10 minutes everyday. You will become happier and healthier and you will add more years to your life.

9   When you hate others and stop sharing your love and knowledge with others, you begin to die spiritually. Remember that

you take nothing from this world when you die, the only thing that goes with you are your good deeds. The more you share your love and knowledge with others, the more these multiply many times over and lead to glorification after death.

10   Do not feel hopeless and helpless. Smile and use your courage even in the midst of the storms of life. Look at a lotus flower, it blossoms in the mud. Maintain hope, as it is your beam of light in the darkness and God is your guide in the journey of life. Use your faith and hold his invisible finger and he will walk with you and will take you out safely from all your problems, sufferings, and dangerous situations.

11   Happiness does not come from collecting expensive material possessions or having lots of money. People have interviewed the richest people in the world and many are still unhappy in their life. Happiness is an inner experience, which is only felt when we are in the present and feel the beauty within us and around us. We share love with others and they return that love

to us. We enjoy fun, freedom, and cherish the precious moments of life.

12   When you have great intentions to help others, the universal powers come in different forms to help you complete your higher goals and the mission of your life.

13   There is an order in nature but change is the law of the universe. Remember and realize that changes are happening every second within our body, mind, and environment. Our internal forces are always adjusting to external changes every minute of everyday. Everyone resists changes due to unknown anxieties, fears, and adjustment problems. Change can be good, if we accept it, think positively, and maintain effort; then we can grow to our full potential and achieve what were once seen as difficult and unattainable goals.

14   Ego, anger, greed, money, land, lust, and attachment are the causes of all evil and destruction in this world. If you can control your mind, senses, and desires,

you can conquer impossible things in life and avoid troubles.

15   When some inauspicious things happen around you or you have unusual dreams, then be aware that something negative is going to happen soon. These are the messages and guidance from the angels around you. Immediately stop and pray, and request God, the universe, and your angels to help and protect you from the upcoming problems or request that the impact of those negative things be reduced, be it unwanted troubles, loss or accidents. You will be surprised that God hears your prayers and helps you in your time of need.

16   The important things to see and feel :
-       God is everywhere
-       Everything is temporary and mortal
-       Death is unavoidable
-       Goodness- when you have purity in your heart and clarity in your thoughts, your speech, actions, and deeds, it reflects that goodness for

others to see and you see goodness in everyone and in everything.

- Beauty- It is all over and around us. It depends on your mood and level of awareness. If you are negative inside, you perceive ugliness outside.

17 The simplest paths to reach God:
- True and pure love
- Meditation
- Serving the poor, homeless, handicapped, elderly, and sick people
- Increasing spiritual awareness among others
- Healing and helping others selflessly

18 The blissful experience that comes through love is:
- Whatever you do, do it with love
- Whoever you meet, greet with love
- Wherever you go, share your love
- Remove the darkness of hate with the light of love.

19   Anger and disease are greater enemies than a human enemy. Anger causes heat in your body, raises your blood pressure, and may cause a heart attack, stroke, or disease. Visualize and remove the cause of your anger from your subconscious mind. Use love, calmness, and forgiveness to overcome your anger. Whenever you encounter a rough person or a tough situation, immediately take 3 deep breaths and use positive affirmations saying, "I will let this go", otherwise you will add another brick of bad experience to the wall of hate and resentment in your subconscious mind. Remember that your anger does not change the situation or the other person. It fuels the fire and affects your relationship with the other person. In the end, it only hurts you, not to the other person, and causes mental and physical illness. Eliminate your anger by writing your emotions and bad experiences on a piece of paper, read it several times and become aware of everything you have stored in your subconscious mind, then throw it into fire. Do this before your anger ruins your relationships and destroy your health and career.

20   Children are the future of tomorrow. Parents have to be good role models for their children. Children do whatever they watch or hear from their parents as home is the first school and parents are the best teachers of their children. Sow the seeds of love, kindness, peace, and tolerance towards others who are different from them. When children grow up with good teachings they make choices and take actions to build a strong society and a great nation.

21   If you want your wishes to come true then look at the first bright star in the southwest area of the sky every evening. Gaze at the star lovingly, smile, and then close your eyes and visualize the star and make your wish with a pure heart and send it to that star in the universe. Wait for a positive result for a few days or weeks; if you still do not see an answer to your wish, then try the same technique for 3 days in a row and wait for a result. Do not be impatient, remember that good things happen when we least expect them.

22   No marriage is perfect as two individuals are not exactly the same. They come from a different family, caste, different religion and philosophy of life, different chemistry (solar and lunar energy), different intelligence levels, expectations, experiences of life, education background, different habits, attitude, and behaviors, different strengths and weaknesses, different character and qualities, different professions and skills and ways of raising children.

23   The universe was created with a sound and that sound was AUM. AUM means creation, sustenance, and destruction. Aum is the most simple and powerful mantra, which lies with each incoming and outgoing breath; you simply have to be aware of it and feel it in your throat and heart.

24   A husband and wife are similar to two wings of a bird, which cannot fly perfectly high without both wings. Perfection in marriage comes when the relationship is given the highest priority

over everything and nurtured with love, care, and attention.

25 The foundations of a good marriage are: love, respect, trust, appreciation, gentleness, and support.

26 Life becomes meaningful when we understand the needs, feelings, and problems of others. We take initiative to help, touch their hearts, and reduce the sufferings of their life.

27 When you have great intentions to help others and you do good things for others selflessly, then good things will happen to you sooner or later in life.

28 Health is order; disease is disorder. A body is healthy when the mind is healthy and the mind is healthy when there is a balance in the major areas/activities of life such as food, sleep, sex, recreation, and relaxation and there is harmony in the living and work environment.

29   Before you teach something to others, first analyze yourself to see whether you have the same bad habit or not. If you do, quit doing that habit first, then use that experience to educate or teach others. Impart your knowledge to others only if you intend to follow what you teach.

30   The four purposes of Human life:
1.   Dharma- Duty to help, serve and protect the family and country
2.   Artha - what we choose to accumulate such as wealth, possessions, land, and knowledge
3.   Kama- Lust and pleasure
4.   Moksha- Enlightenment and freedom from rebirth. The secret of inner peace and happiness is to be free of desires and attachment. I own nothing, I have a free will.

31   The success of a man or woman, company, society, government nations, civilization, and the world, depends on the unity of people, moral religious and political leaders, insightful vision, creative thinking, creative actions, right decisions, concise and clear

communication, courage, enthusiasm, right attitude, patience, honesty, good planning, compassionate service, team work, hard work and networking.

"Peace on earth cannot be achieved without inner peace, love, trust, tolerance and acceptance of others. When we change, the world changes."

May peace prevail on earth.

Inner reflections, progress and resolutions for New Year

ABOUT THE AUTHOR

Raj Kumar lives with his wife Sunita and daughter Sapna in Hawaii. In 1998, after his heart surgery, he opened a healing center called-New Life Center in Hawaii. He practices as an Ayurvedic wellness counselor, Reiki master, Palmist, Hypnotherapist, Yoga and meditation teacher. He has been a guest on Radio and TV. He has given lectures on stress management, Pranayama, Religion, meditation in the hospitals, colleges and universities in different countries. He has contributed articles on child abuse, weight loss through Ayurveda, stress management through Pranayama, yoga and meditation to Magazines and newspapers. He has received recognition from the Presidents of the United States of America, Bill Clinton and George W. Bush. He is the director of American-Indian friendship council in Hawaii. He has already published two Books -"From Darkness To Light" and "The Secrets of Health and Healing". His books are available at Authorhouse.com, BarnesandNoble.com and Amazon.com.

For more information about Raj Kumar's books and services E-mail:

Cosmicyoga@verizon.net

Website: www.cosmicyoga.net

Also by Raj Kumar, Ph.D.

From Darkness to Light
A Treasure of Inspirational Thoughts on Spiritual Living

The Secrets of Health & Healing
Heal Your Body, Mind and Spirit through Ancient Wisdom, Methods and Techniques

Printed in the United States
39821LVS00001B/22-120